PREFACE.

THIS series of Albums contains some of the shorter pieces of modern Russian pianoforte music, which should be found useful in our schools. The Albums are numbered in the order of their difficulty. Books I. and II. contain pieces in the easier major and minor keys, and deal with simple rhythms. Books III. and IV. deal with more varied rhythms, make a greater demand on the imagination, and require more experience and facility in the use of the pedals. Books V. and VI. contain some characteristic examples of modern Russian music, but the pieces in Book VI. are too difficult for any but the very musical.

Although, in making the selection, I have had a definite educational end in view, I have tried to include in this collection only such pieces as have a distinct musical value. This was, of course, far more difficult in the case of Books I. and II. than in the case of the later Books; yet I venture to think that there are pieces even in the earlier Books that will give pleasure. Modern harmonies, seven-bar phrases, interesting extensions of sentences, and unusual rhythmic figures all play their part in giving a distinct charm to some of the simplest pieces; while in the more difficult ones there is the added interest of noting either the foreign influences under which modern Russian music has fallen, or the strong nationalist tendency which marks the music of such a composer as Zolotarev.

With regard to my work as editor, I have confined myself as a rule to fingering and pedalling the greater number of the pieces. In the case of the Novellettes of Maykapar in Books II., III., and IV., and the Prelude by Goedicke in Book VI., this has been done by the composer: for the other pieces I am responsible. The pedalling, however, is not intended to be exhaustive; the experienced teacher must supplement it, since the exigences of the printer forbid the insertion of many directions necessary for dealing with the subtleties and complexities of modern music. Nevertheless, I venture to hope that my suggestions may prevent the young student from falling into grave mistakes, and that, in the earlier Books, the hints I have given may serve to show how the pedal may be used to advantage, even by beginners.

The use of the pedal plays such an important part in modern pianoforte playing that, in my opinion, it cannot be taught too soon; and my experience as a teacher has shown me that it is quite possible to teach it thoroughly and systematically in our schools.

If acquaintance with these smaller pieces should lead teachers to make a more comprehensive study of Russian music, the purpose of this collection will have been achieved.

ANNIE T. WESTON.

LONDON, 1916

No 1.

Petite Pièce.

A. Goedicke.
Op. 6. No 14.

N B The Pedal is indicated thus: ℘ and lasts, failing the usual sign (*) for its removal, till the following ℘

№ 2.

Miniature.

A. Goedicke.
Op. 8. № 2.

rallentando   *al*   *fine*

No 3.
Chansonnette.

N. Amani.
Op. 15. No 3.

№ 4.
Canzonetta.

S. Pantchenko.
Op. 17. № 1.

Nº 5.

Chanson Russe.

K. Eiges.
Op. 6. Nº 5.

Allegro moderato.

Fingered and pedalled
by the Composer.

№ 6.
Toccattina.

S. Maykapar.
Op. 8. № 1.

№ 7.
Pastorale.

Fingered and pedalled
by the Composer.

S. Maykapar.
Op. 8. № 3.

Nº 8.

Chèz le forgeron.

S. Maykapar.
Op. 8. Nº 5.

Allegretto sostenuto e preciso. ♩=76.

Fingered and pedalled
by the Composer.

№ 9.

Berceuse.

S. Maykapar.
Op. 8. № 6.

Allegretto dolcissimo. ♩♩.=88.

pp sempre *pp* e una corda

poco cresc.

Nº 10.

Pièce enfantine.

S. Maykapar.
Op. 4. Nº 3.

Nº 11.

Romance.

R. Glière.
Op. 31. Nº 7.

№ 12.

Chant des moissonneuses.

(Polish Folk-Song.)

H. Pachulski.
Op. 23. № 12.

№ 13.

Allegro.

N. Ladoukhin.
Op. 10. № 11.